"Either write something worth reading or do something worth writing."

—Benjamin Franklin

Teaching High School Creative Writing

L.A. Detwiler

Published by L.A. Detwiler, 2022.

While every precaution has been taken in the preparation of this book, the publisher assumes no responsibility for errors or omissions, or for damages resulting from the use of the information contained herein.

TEACHING HIGH SCHOOL CREATIVE WRITING

First edition. April 9, 2022.

Copyright © 2022 L.A. Detwiler.

ISBN: 979-8201247546

Written by L.A. Detwiler.

Table of Contents

Introduction 1

Strategy One: Put down the red pen. 5

Strategy Two: Create a positive atmosphere where students feel safe to be themselves. 11

Strategy Three: How to Structure Your Curriculum and Class 19

Strategy Four: Where to find activities and ideas 31

Strategy Five: Recognize Your Strengths and Weaknesses 41

Strategy Six: Creating effective critique circles is crucial 46

Strategy Seven: How to tackle writer's block 57

Strategy Eight: Talk about your own writing in order to encourage your students. 62

Strategy Nine: Creativity isn't always found with a paper and pencil. 66

Strategy Ten: Celebrate students' successes. 71

Strategy Eleven: Focus on Growth, Not Mastery 76

A Final Word: The Power of Creative Writing: Inspiration for You 81

Fun Prompts for Students to Answer 84

Story Starters 86

About the Author 88

Lindsay's Books | Sweet Romance.................................89

Thriller/Horror 91

Poetry 92

To all of those with a writing dream; I hope you chase it fearlessly and know your voice needs to be heard.

Introduction

Excited.

Honored.

Almost vomiting.

If you're reading this book, I'm going to assume the following:

1. You've been granted or tasked with teaching a creative writing course at your high school, summer camp, or even a higher education institute.
2. You are feeling at least one if not all of the above emotions.
3. You're looking for advice on where to start.

The reason I'm willing to bet these three things are true is because I was you about seven years ago. When I got the chance to take over our high school creative writing program in my third year of teaching, I felt all of the above emotions–but mostly the vomiting emotion.

It wasn't that I felt incapable of teaching writing. Writing had been my passion for as long as I could remember–it was why I became an English teacher. I'd spent years of my childhood filling notebooks with made-up tales of fluffy bunnies, talking parrots, and everything in between (usually involving an animal or ten). In addition, when I was granted the opportunity to take over the classes, I'd already been published several times.

Still, there's something about being given the reins to a creative class that is daunting. For one, most of us teachers like structure, organization, and a methodical plan. With creative writing class, I found none of that in place. There isn't a set structure to teaching a subjective topic like creative writing. The mere subject matter itself makes a scope and sequence difficult to map out. Furthermore, there are very few resources out there for high school creative writing teachers, probably because it isn't a commonly taught class (thanks, standardized testing, right?). And although it feels great to set down the English teacher textbook and finally focus on creativity, where do you even begin knowing what to actually teach? The state standards offer little structure or help, giving vague hints about style and voice. Still, what should a high school class focus on? How should students be assessed? How do you teach someone to be creative?

These were all questions I struggled with in my first few years of teaching the course. How did I sort it out? Trial and error, mostly. I made mistakes. I restructured. I tried new activities and abandoned some old ones. And eventually, over the years, I created a class that felt right. It's a class where I love to be–and so do my students, for the most part. It's a class where I feel like they're learning what they need to know for the field but still have freedom to make choices and be themselves. It's a class with assessments and direct instruction but different in the sense the kids aren't smothered by expectations of mastery. In a sense, it's a free-flowing class that still offers a sense of structure and expectations.

Today, I not only have Creative Writing One class that I teach and developed, but I have Level Two and a Novel Writing course. Since that first class, I've also become a USA Today Bestselling author. Still, even now, the thing I love about teaching creative writing is that no two classes are ever the same. The thing you'll learn in this book, hopefully, is that there isn't a one-size-fits-all approach to teaching creative writing. It ebbs and flows. It transforms as you change, too.

Still, in this book, I hope to give you practical tips for starting up your own creative writing class or curriculum. I'll talk about tried-and-true strategies that have worked for me in the classroom, basic tenants to use in your own class, and activities I've enjoyed. We'll talk about how to establish grading standards that give you flexibility and how to organize your class to maximize learning while still letting students have options. I'll talk about how to create a helpful critique environment where students feel comfortable growing.

I wrote this book for a few reasons. Other books out there focus either solely on activities or exclusively on writing theory. I didn't feel like there was a book out there for "real" teachers–teachers who face the challenges of time, behavior, and pressure. I wanted to write a book from the heart, in a way, one that speaks to my own successes and learning curves. Most of all, I wanted to write a book in the hopes of inspiring you to create your own favorite class–because my creative writing class is my breath of fresh air during the day. When done well, your creative writing class can become a safe haven not only for your students to learn how to express themselves, but for you to be the kind of teacher I think we all want to be. It might not feel like it now. You might be feeling overwhelmed and like vomiting. But I promise, if you read this book and then make the ideas your own, you'll shine.

And let me say this, right at the beginning. It doesn't matter how skilled you are in writing or how fancy your prompts are. It doesn't matter if you have basic prompts or elaborate schemes. It doesn't matter if you have technology or yellow wooden pencils to work with. It doesn't matter if you can afford to take your class to the Globe Theater or if you barely have a broom closet to teach out of. None of that is needed to be a successful creative writing teacher, which is perhaps what I love the most.

I'm going to tell you the underlying secret to success now so you can keep it in mind the whole book. Sure, the other tips are nice and can be helpful. But at the core of your writing class, if you can keep this one thing in mind, you'll be just fine. You'll be more than fine–you'll be wildly successful.

The secret?

Make the students feel safe enough to be seen, and you've won.

The rest is just filler.

Lindsay (L.A.) Detwiler

Strategy One: Put down the red pen.

What matters most?

Over the years, numerous students have sat in my creative writing class desks and penned all sorts of works. My class is a mix of tenth through twelfth graders of all different abilities and levels. Some students dream of publishing a novel. Some have already started. Several take the class because they want to get better at writing. A few follow their friends. Still others end up in my class because it's the only course that fits in their schedule, and it was either that or stay back another year.

All types of students and writers sit in my class with all different starting levels–that became apparent from day one. Thus, I found myself asking very early on in my teaching days the question posed above: What matters most?

As an English teacher, I'd been taught that grammar is crucial to success, and we have to model appropriate grammar for our kids at all times. I can remember my student teacher mentor blasting me for using an improper form of a word during teaching one time. Thus, in the writing classroom, it can be difficult to let go of the notion that misspellings and typos must be corrected.

One of my favorite books to share excerpts from, *The Road* by Cormac McCarthy, demonstrates a harsh truth English teachers seldom recognize; in certain periods of time, grammar is superfluous. His apocalyptic novel uses minimal punctuation and almost no dialogue marks. In this dog-eat-dog world, the story is what matters, not the restrictions of grammar.

Thus, in my creative writing class, I follow this bare-bones lead. This is because when I asked the question about what mattered in my class, it was clear to me what my answer was:

Creativity.

Confidence.

Voice.

These were the things I wanted my kids to leave with, no matter how they came to me. I wanted my students to learn to be imaginative and take risks in their ideas. The only bad idea was a boring one; I wanted them to be brave and come up with new concepts that really had no other place in their academic day. I wanted to take advantage of the freedom I had without standardized testing, and I wanted to pass those benefits on to them.

Most classrooms in a school setting don't have the luxury of stepping away from rigid state requirements and high-stakes testing. Thus, most of my students don't get the opportunity to explore creativity at its finest—the kind that sometimes works and sometimes doesn't. They've been programmed to tirelessly seek the "correct" answer and perfect their grades, thus, arguably stifling their imaginations. I wanted my classroom to be a place that felt different than other classes, not because we are kicking back and doing nothing but because it was a place they were free to take risks, make mistakes, and still get applauded. I wanted my writing class to focus on content generation and ideas, not perfecting English concepts.

I also wanted them to learn confidence. Many of my best creative writing students struggle with grammar, spelling, and the traditional English classroom. They are used to getting papers back that look like they've been massacred—red pen highlighting every single mistake. "You can't," these red etchings say to them. Many of them have come to believe those markings, have taken them on as scars.

Thus, I made a quick decision in year one that grammar and spelling wouldn't affect grades in my writing class. I do not have a red pen in that class. I do not correct apostrophes or misspellings. We highlight tense changes because that is part of the writing guidelines, and we talk about how too many run-ons or fragments can get in the way of a message. Other than that, I don't make note of anything else. This is not the class to analyze commas in a compound sentence or the proper use of a semicolon.

The result, I've found, is that voices once stifled are able to rise above their limitations. Students who struggle with grammar shed the weight of "you can't" vibes and let their own voices ring out. They tell their stories, unencumbered by a lack of vocabulary or understanding of syntax. They let their truths shine and showcase vulnerabilities that otherwise would have been hidden. They learn early on their voices matter more than any red pen.

Won't ignoring grammar mistakes make it difficult for you to read and grade their works appropriately? I'll cover this in a later chapter, but in my class, almost all of the grading is done through read alouds. This not only makes your task as a grader more efficient, but it also helps the students to learn from each other. They internalize the learning on a whole different level.

Most of all, though, this approach helps the students learn what I think the class should be all about, at least in an introductory level: they learn confidence. Suddenly, the "You can't" message becomes "You can." I have seen the genuine smiles of students who have only ever had their writing corrected beam brightly when they're given compliments on their ideas. I've come to learn, too, that you can't fix grammar in isolation. Once students have the confidence in their writing and in their story, only then does grammar even matter. When they understand they have a story worth telling, then you can begin to tackle the complex, abstract issues of how poor grammar detracts from their message. If they don't truly believe they have words worth sharing, why would it matter if a few commas or improperly placed modifiers detract from the meaning?

This is, of course, not the way you have to run your creative writing classroom. The beautiful thing about this subject and course is there are countless ways of teaching it in a beneficial way. Maybe you'll decide to hold onto the red pen just a little bit, or maybe you'll put it on reserve for later in the course. Maybe the grammar stickler in you won't let you loosen the grip. Still, I challenge you to at least put the red pen down for a few months and see what progress you can make on content creation. I think once you see for yourself the impact you can have by taking the perfectionist pressure off your writers, you'll understand the benefits firsthand. You'll start to hear ideas and creativity I would argue you wouldn't otherwise.

Eventually, if you feel the need to focus on grammar, consider focusing on grammar issues that publishers commonly note finding in manuscripts. Some of the issues I've worked through with editors include:

- Overusing the word "that"

- Overusing adverbs

- Not using enough action verbs

- Using tell instead of show

- Overusing the word "very"

- Repeated words in close proximity

If you tackle grammar from a publishing/style perspective instead of a technical perspective, students understand it in a more meaningful way. They have a reason to clean up some of their usage and begin to realize how these small changes impact their wording, impact, and voice

The Takeaway:

- Avoid making your creative writing class "another English class." Instead, promote freedom of ideas by ignoring grammar mistakes, at least in the beginning.

● Promoting content generation and creativity are skills that serve all learners in the long run. Most students don't get to practice these in a low-pressure environment, so make your class a place to explore.

● Focus on what students are doing well in order to build confidence.

● Establish a "you can" attitude about writing before you teach the students to take ownership for more complex concepts such as grammar.

Strategy Two: Create a positive atmosphere where students feel safe to be themselves.

To write is to be vulnerable.

If you've written anything from a novel to a poem to a letter to a social media post, you know the veracity of this statement. Whether we're writing truth or fiction, a piece of who we are always works its way into our prose. The way we view the world, our background, and what we value comes out in all sorts of obvious and subtle ways. Thus, in order to really put ourselves on the page and have the confidence to share it, we need to feel safe: safe in who we are, safe in our community, and safe in sharing our words.

If you want your creative writing class to be successful and meaningful, you have to build that sense of community for your students.

I realize this is no small feat, truly, especially in the world of education we are living in. Pulled in so many directions with statistics and data seeming to drive all decisions, we often feel like we don't have the capability to connect. Add to the obvious disconnect many of us see in our students thanks to technology and other factors, and it can feel like an insurmountable hurdle.

Here's the thing, though: the creative writing classroom gives you more hope and opportunity to build that safe space for your students than perhaps any other class. The nature of creative writing begets connection and emotion. It's about feeling things and expressing those feelings. It's about finding ways to forge ahead with human connection. You, writing teacher, hold the advantage in your building or school because you have the opportunity to build the sort of rapport and community the teacher textbooks like to talk about, the kinds that seem to be some fantastical *Narnia* of teaching.

It does take time, though. You have to unpeel the shells of your students, who have often been hardened by the education system itself, the trials of high school, and the difficulties of a harsh world. There is sometimes a tendency for students to mistrust educators because their experiences have only been negative. There will also be a hesitancy to open up to each other; vulnerability takes courage. However, if you can take initiative to encourage connection at the beginning of your class, everything you teach and learn from a writing perspective will reach new heights.

I've seen this in my own classes over the years. Each year, the class starts out as cold, quiet, and aloof. No one really talks to each other. Everyone is terrified of the prospect of sharing. But, as the weeks go on and with carefully constructed activities, there is a general loosening up. Students realize I wasn't kidding when I told them it was a very different kind of class. They relax into the relative freedom of the course. Creative writing class, for me, isn't about oppression and rules. It's about exploration and adventure. Certainly, we are still bound by the general confines of adequate school behavior. Respect, showing up on time, taking care of school property—the usual rules still apply. But there aren't harsh rubrics or do-or-die directions for assignments. Students can ask to modify projects to fit their needs. They pick their seats. They listen to music on their earbuds as they write. The atmosphere I seek to create is one of relaxation and escape from the pressures of the school day. Still, there is work to be done, and they know this.

There will be students who try to push the boundaries from time to time—they are teenagers, after all. There are guidelines, there are grades, and there are expectations. But for me, at the forefront of the class is seeing them as individuals. It's in getting to know them and getting them to know each other. My focus is on connection instead of content.

I know that if you've never taught a writing class, this sounds like a magical yet made-up version of reality. In a school system that is pressurized at the core, it can feel impossible to tackle this free-flowing spirit and actually realize it in the walls of the school building.

You'll have to trust me on this. And, once you see it unfold for yourself, I think you'll begin to understand the truly addictive magic of creative writing class and why it's my favorite to teach.

So how do you actually go about building the sense of community we want for our writers? As I said, it takes time. You can't rush it, and a lot of it is up to the students.

I start by explaining this very concept during our first meeting. We discuss the idea of vulnerability and how every writer needs a safe space to explore their ideas. We converse about what respect and support looks like in a writing classroom and what it doesn't. I also make it very clear what they all take out of the class is in their hands. If they can create a genuine environment where people value honesty and trust, we will all grow as writers. If they don't take the time to do that, the class essentially falls apart.

From there, it's a slow progression of getting to know each other. We do a lot of ice breaker games at the beginning. These admittedly cheesy getting to know you activities, though, are crucial. Students need to understand and respect their differences in writing and personalities for the class to work. We play a beach ball game where students toss around a beach ball I've written questions on with permanent marker to get to know each other. We do a lot of sharing about our likes, dislikes, hopes, and dreams. We also do several activities where they let us learn about who they are. These can take any form you choose, from a writing to even a collage. The key is that students are getting to know each other beyond just surface level.

I also start out with a free choice writing at the beginning, tasking students with the duty of letting us know who they are as writers. This also allows them to get past that first nervous hurdle of: Here's who I am as a writer. This is an intimidating process for anyone, and especially those in high school, so I always make sure they have plenty of time to perfect this first writing. I want them to be proud and confident of the first piece they write so they can get up in front of the class with a bit more ease.

Your mood and approach as a teacher is also crucial to the environment. I try to take as much time as I can, especially in the early days, just talking to them. We talk about fun *Would you rather?* questions. I get challenging, deep questions off Pinterest and we discuss them. I have them write questions for everyone in the class to answer. These conversations are what truly build the connections and the laughs along the way.

Humor is also really helpful for getting everyone out of their shell. My writing classes always seem to share in my quirky, introverted nature, and our sense of humor typically lines up. My best writing classes always have a slew of inside jokes that we fall back on and banter about, which also helps with the sense of community.

It is crucial as well that no one feels left out. For some students, your writing class will be completely out of their comfort zone, and they might want to hide. Certainly don't put them on the spot in the first day or two, but ease them into the class. Make sure they know you see them. Make it a point to sit by them and talk to them for a few minutes.

None of it is revolutionary or crazy complex tactics. Most of building your community in your class is about two things: time and seeing your students. Really, truly seeing them.

If your students know you recognize them, that they aren't invisible, and that they are safe to be who they are in the walls of your classroom, then you've won.

Once your class settles into a sense of community and comfort, you can expect their writings to become more vulnerable. I've had students share really hard, difficult life experiences in their work. Always praise and honor their willingness to be open in class. Always make sure your students understand what a big deal it is for someone to be genuine in their work and to take the time to share it.

This can be scary as an educator. What if students share something exceptionally painful or tragic? How should you handle it? As a writer myself, I know the power of writing in helping to heal. As a writing teacher, you should be prepared for this openness and honesty. It inarguably can put a lot of weight on your shoulders as an educator, especially when you realize how much pain some of your students are going through. Don't forget you don't have to shoulder that alone. Make sure you have a good relationship with your guidance counselors, and don't be afraid to lean on them for support. Also, I always err on the side of caution. If a student shares something difficult, deep, or painful, I go to guidance about it just for a check in. I discuss the possibility with my students on the first day of the class. They know they need to write pieces that are appropriate (i.e. they cannot write about any other students in the school or something that could be perceived as a threat). They also know that if they share something deep, I may be required to turn it into guidance. I make it clear this does not mean they are in trouble; it simply means they might be checked on, which is a good thing.

To me, one of the most rewarding parts of teaching creative writing is the opportunity to give students a safe space to express their truest selves, even when that comes with pain and hardship. I also think there is such a benefit to students understanding each other's story on a deeper level. One of the most important lessons I've learned as an educator is you never truly understand someone's whole story by looking at them or talking to them surface-level. The creative writing course allows us to really delve into that ideal and hopefully change students' perspectives on each other, on what it means to be human, and on how writing can help us empathize with each other.

The Takeaway:

- The most important thing you can do in the early days of your course is to build trust and safety.

- Getting to know your students and helping them really know each other is your main goal in the first few weeks if not the whole class.

- Praise and recognize vulnerability. Teach students about the power of writing to help process hard things.

- When you are handling tough situations that come up in writing class, go to guidance for expert help. Don't shoulder all of the emotions on your own.

- Creating a safe environment is a unique gift of creative writing class. Few other places in the school afford instructors the flexibility and capabilities of creating a community-like feel. Celebrate the opportunity, even when it feels difficult.

● The most important thing you can do as a writing teacher is to see every student for who they are, appreciate who they are, and take the time to get to know them. Your skill level doesn't matter as much as your willingness to do this.

Strategy Three: How to Structure Your Curriculum and Class

I'm betting for many of you reading this book, figuring out what to teach and how is what actually brought you here. When I first started the class, I really struggled to find resources on what I should be teaching for a full-year course. There were plenty of fun activities to sprinkle in my class but no real guide to what students should leave my room knowing.

In this strategy, we'll break down what you should teach and how you should structure your class. I want to be clear, though—there truly is no one-size-fits-all approach. How and what you teach will depend on:

- The students in front of you

- Your experience level

- What interests the students the most

- If they've done any creative writing or not

- How many days you have together

This can change from year to year as well. My class never looks exactly the same year to year. Still, this book will give you guidelines of the skills and topics I've come to believe are the most important for students to know. These decisions come from not only my experience as a writing teacher but also as a published author. My time in the publishing industry has helped me really understand what is most helpful for my students to know when they leave my class and what the industry favors.

This is not to say writing to be published is the only writing of value. Thus, I also make sure I cover important skills dealing with creativity and thinking outside of the box. Sometimes, traditional publishing seeks to stifle thinking that goes beyond the business equation for book sales, but that's a discussion for another time.

Know that you can and should tweak my ideas to fit your own needs. This should be a springboard for your own values and structure. Still, I think it is helpful to understand what a full course can look like as you decide how to build your own.

How should I structure my class?

This was the most difficult decision I made when I first took over our creative writing class. Because creative writing is rarely a tested element of standardized testing, it often takes a backseat in classrooms and standards. Thus, it was difficult to even know what students should learn. I drew on my own experiences as a writer and an author to answer the question.

Really, there are two ways to organize your content you teach. You could teach a writing class based on medium or based on skills.

Structure by Medium

A class based on medium teaches students based on the types of creative writing. For example, your units could look like this:

- The short story

- Drama/play writing

- Poetry

- Children's Literature

- Creative nonfiction

In this type of class, your focus is on the final product for each unit. I taught ninth grade for one year, and our creative writing workshop was structured this way. There are, of course, benefits and downfalls to running a class in this type of organization.

The benefits are that the students get exposed to every type of creative writing. They learn a wide array of skills and are pushed outside of their comfort zone at times. It also is a great exploratory sort of class for students who have done little writing and don't really know what they prefer. There is also little chance the class will feel repetitive since the change of medium does wonders for interest level.

One negative to this structure is that students potentially only get to shine for a tiny piece of the class, which can stilt their confidence. If you have a poet who takes your class, they only get to feel like an expert in one of the five units. Certainly, pushing students outside of their comfort zone is a helpful and important skill. However, if you have reluctant writers or students who lack confidence in their work, this structure can reinforce their negative self views.

Additionally, when I taught this structure, I found that my attention was pulled in so many directions. As the teacher, I was trying to master all of the genres, many of which I myself am not as strong at. I was trying to become an expert at these five very different mediums, which is a tall and overwhelming task. I found at the end of the course I felt like I had just given them a surface-level look at the medium without real, actionable skills.

This structure can work well for your class if you:

- Want to do an exploration with your students of all mediums to find what they prefer

- Are willing to do a lot of research and potentially bring in a lot of experts to cover any areas you don't feel confident

- Want to cover a lot of ground or have a whole year course to fill

Skills-Based Organization

In this type of organization, the skills become the focus of the units. Students typically focus on short stories as their medium for exploring the skills, but you can also incorporate other mediums to fit different skill sets. Students also are offered some flexibility. Poets, for example, are able to write poetry for various activities as they see fit.

The skills I cover are listed below. This list was designed by me based on what I felt were crucial skills for students to learn and what the industry seemed to mark as important.

Creative Writing Level I:

- Characterization
  - Developing quirks in characters
  - Creating realistic characters who readers root for
  - Writing villains
  - Using antagonists to strengthen your characterization

- Dialogue
  - Writing dialogue that flows
  - Using dialogue as a storytelling technique
  - Using dialogue to reveal characterization

- Descriptive Writing
  - Show vs. Tell
  - Using imagery to bring your work to life
  - The power of verbs

○ The use of setting to support a story

● General Creativity

○ Various activities to promote creative thinking

○ Challenges presented to students to help them learn to work under pressure

○ Writer's block activities

○ This topic is covered in a later chapter

Creative Writing Level II

● Advanced Characterization

○ The use of minor characters

○ Manipulating point of view to reveal characterization

● Plot

○ Effective plot devices

○ Building suspense

○ Using foreshadowing to create engaging stories

○ Plot twists

● Publishing

○ Author studies

- ○ Publishing tips

- ○ Query letters

- ○ Social media for authors

- ● Science Fiction

- ○ World Building

- ○ Building fantasy characters

- ○ Creating world systems that are believable

The benefits to a skills-based curriculum are that students focus on building the creative writing skills needed to be successful and practice them in various mediums. There is a definite sense of organization to the class, and students get to be challenged while still focusing on their medium of choice. I alternate small and long-term assignments to keep the class engaging and throw in some fun, creative activities to break up the class (See Strategy 8). I feel like my students leave my class well-rounded and well-versed in the skill sets needed by professionals in the field. I also feel like this strategy gives us flexibility to adjust the curriculum based on the needs of students. If they are great at worldbuilding, we might spend more time on characterization, or vice versa. We really focus on strengthening them as writers in their chosen medium.

The negatives are that sometimes students can fall into a rut if you let them. Comfortable with short stories, for example, they may never venture into drama writing or poetry. Furthermore, students who really don't write very often might not know what medium to choose and get frustrated. Finally, if you focus too much on the skills, there is a risk this class will become a second English class where you are so focused on checking tasks off lists that you forget to let the curriculum breathe.

Whichever method you choose, I think it's crucial you remember to let students be who they are and also challenge them when you can. It's a balancing act of building their confidence in their chosen area of writing and pushing them outside of their comfort zone to explore. I think either structure can be successful as long as you keep this in mind.

How to Teach Your Class: What the Lessons Look Like

Now that you've picked your curriculum structure, you might be wondering: What will a typical week of lesson plans look like in this class?

It can be jarring to plan for this sort of class at first. Without the strict structure that builds on itself of our typical subject curriculums, we can sometimes flounder with the freedom. Should we have tests as assessments? How should assignments be graded? How should you deliver the information?

Again, this choice will depend on who you are as a teacher and the students in front of you. Here are some of the tips I've learned along the way, though, and the lesson plan structure I follow.

Typical unit structure

For me, this class has always been a student-centered class. The typical unit in this class looks like this:

- Introduce our concept with a lecture, handouts from authors, and tips for the topic. I sometimes also use videos, Nearpods, etc. to get the information across

- We do a practice activity or two—smaller, low-pressure activities to build on the skills I've introduced. These could be a paragraph writing, an activity done with a partner, a group write, etc.

- After they are comfortable with the information, we do a longer, week-long writing project. These are sometimes prompted and sometimes free choice.

- We share our work and critique.

- I do some sort of a fun game or activity before moving to the next unit.

It should be noted this structure isn't rigid. When the kids are feeling bored or blah, I mix in one of my creative activities. I never want the class to feel repetitive or like they're simply coming in, writing, and then reading their work. I like to keep them guessing because I think variety keeps the creativity flowing.

Assessment

I do not give quizzes or tests in Creative Writing. This is a personal choice. For me, I am more concerned that they can put the material to use in their own writing and not memorize it for a multiple choice test. Their grades in this class come solely from writing. Typically, our smaller practice assignments are graded for completion. I've already discussed in strategy one my philosophy of grammar with regards to creative writing. Thus, the practice activities are graded for completion only.

The final writing is graded according to a rubric. I make these based on the skills we are discussing. I have also used a creative writing rubric from my state that I found on my state education website. Regardless, the rubric is meant to be very positive. I rarely take off many points in level one writing. My students know that as long as they are trying, growing, and using the tips we've discussed, their grade isn't something to worry about. I think if you want to stifle creative writers, make them nervous about grades. Make them feel like they have to put on a performance in their writing to please you. It is when we have this stress that our creativity typically goes out the window. I do not want that for my students.

I grade their assignments as they share. I don't look at their work because again, grammar doesn't matter. I don't want them to feel nervous about that. I also like to hear them read their own work so I know what they think is important and how they are interpreting their words. I ask follow-up questions at the end so I can really understand what they were going for and how much work they put into their thought process. This helps me assess their growth.

I also suggest keeping students' writings from the beginning of the class. One of my favorite activities is to give them back their very first writing on the last day of class. I love to see them realize how much they've grown in the class, even when they haven't thought they did. This is a very validating assessment and, in my opinion, the only one that actually matters even though it isn't graded.

My class is an elective at our school, so I do not give homework. I always give plenty of time for assignments to be completed in class. Students only have homework if they do not use their class time wisely or want to spend extra time on an assignment. I am never in a rush in my class to get through the curriculum; if we need more time on a unit, we take it.

Again, the biggest piece of advice I can give you is to not let the class become stagnant through expectations and patterns. It is easy to fall into a teach, write, share pattern, which can become very humdrum quickly. Use the element of surprise. Offer up random, challenging prompts. Play games. Do fun activities here and there. Enjoy the fact that you aren't on a strict time schedule and do what you are good at: teach.

The Takeaways:

- Decide whether or not to use a medium based or skills-based organization

• Variety is key with both methods.

• Let students shine in their area of expertise but also push them out of their comfort zone when you can.

• Be flexible. Each class might have different needs and interests. Adjust your activities and schedule accordingly.

• Consider being lenient with your assessment. Focus on growth and effort, not necessarily perfection (What is a perfect writer, anyway?)

• Have fun. Really. Kids who are excited to come to your class and enjoy the atmosphere will be more creative and, thus, more productive writers.

Strategy Four: Where to find activities and ideas

The beautiful thing about teaching creative writing is that the sky really is the limit when it comes to the activities you can do. Also, you don't need fancy resources to make the class exciting. If you can think up the prompt, your students can be challenged by it. Some days, all the preparation you need is a fun, thought-provoking question.

This book is not a book of activities like most of the resources out there (Stay tuned, though! I'm working on putting together my best writing activities for writing teachers. Additionally, you can find some activities at the end of this book that you can use right now with your writers).

This book is designed to give you the best tips and tricks about the teaching of creative writing, the structure, and tactics to make it work. There are numerous amazing resources out there to give you activity ideas. This chapter will outline the ones I've found to be the best so you don't waste your money and time on resources that are boring, pointless, or not beneficial.

Some of my favorite activities have been self-designed. They are the product of my own creative thinking, oftentimes coming in the middle of the night with a "What if?" sort of question. There really is writing inspiration everywhere, and if you begin to look for it, you'll see that there are writing activities hiding everywhere as well. I challenge you, thus, to try to come up with at least a few of your own activities and prompts throughout the course so you can make it your own. No matter who you are or what writing experience you have (or think you don't have), you are creative, powerful, and intelligent. You have so much to offer your students in ways of challenging them and coming up with exciting, thought-provoking ideas. Don't sell yourself short or discount your own thoughts. By coming up with your own ideas, you'll add your own flair to the class and give your students a unique experience that won't be readily duplicated anywhere else. Furthermore, remember sometimes simple is better. You don't need flashy, wild prompts to inspire greatness in your students. Simple ideas can spark genius.

Still, I know that exhaustion, stress, and time can be limitations on our creativity. Realistically speaking, it can be draining to come up with all your own content. Furthermore, in the first years when self-doubt can creep in, you might wonder if you are teaching activities that are exciting enough, challenging enough, creative enough, or academic enough.

Below, you'll find a list of resources I've found to be helpful, both for me to find activities and to guide the students. I am certainly not endorsed or sponsored by any of these. I simply have found them helpful over the years.

Books for you to use:

Stephen King's On Writing

Yes, there is a lot of profanity in this book. No, I don't care. This book is so well-written and eye-opening. The first half offers inspiration for you and your students. It covers King's rocky rise to fame, which isn't as straight and smooth as one would expect. I love the inspiration in that and how he shares his rejections. I think students need to hear about that.

Furthermore, the last half of the book is filled with expert tips and tricks from King. I felt like it made me feel comfortable with the subject matter before teaching my students. I also use some excerpts from the sections on characterization and description in my class. Any time I can bring other writers' experiences into my classroom, I try to do just that. If nothing else, it is an amazing resource for you to read as a teacher in order to gain a deeper understanding of the writing craft you are teaching.

Don't Forget to Write for the Secondary Grades by 826 National

I bought this book my first year and used quite a few of the creative activities out of the fifty. Some require some prep work and gathering of materials, but some are very simple. It's always helpful to have a few extra activities prepared in case one of yours doesn't work out.

Rip the Page by Karen Benke

Again, this is a great resource to buy for your first year. I found some of the activities to be odd and childish, but there were enough worthwhile writing ideas for me to feel it was a good investment. It's also great to keep in your drawer for anytime the inspiration runs dry.

Writing Journals from Five Below

Five Below has a great stock of writing journals that I like to buy. These have various prompts in them for teen writers. I keep one or two of these at school in case, again, I need quick writing prompt inspiration.

Books for your students:

Anne Lamott's Bird by Bird

One of my former students recommended this to me when she went to college and used it in a class. It is a wonderful breakdown of writing tips that is suitable for high school and undergraduate students. Anne has a very accessible writing style that makes writers really think about what they are doing and why. I loved her quick tips and tricks and felt like I could apply them to my own work easily.

This is a great resource if you want to work on your own expertise before teaching or if your students need more structure to their advice. I also recommend this to students who really want to level up their writing; I use it as extra reading for them. I often use excerpts from Lamott's book for each of my units.

The Road by Cormac McCarthy

First, I love this book. If you are a fan of dystopian novels and poetic prose, read this one. Seriously. But in writing class, I don't use the whole book; I use excerpts. I think McCarthy demonstrates how the juxtaposition of beautiful and dark can work wonderfully in writing. I love his poetic prose coupled with the end-of-the-world bleakness in his story. We look at different passages for world building, description, and characterization.

The Haunting of Hill House by Shirley Jackson

Again, this is another favorite for pulling excerpts. I think to write well, students have to read great writing. This book is an example of stunning description that leaps off the page. It is exciting and well-written, which makes it a prime example to set the stage for quality writing in your class.

Technology/Websites that are helpful:

No Red Ink

We've discussed how I don't love doing grammar in creative writing, but if you feel like you can't resist, this free program is a must. I actually use it in my English classes because the data it provides is amazing. It's an engaging way for students to complete grammar, and I love that it is fully customized to students' needs. You can assign a pre-test to them at the beginning of the unit, and then they get questions based on how they do on the pre-test. Once they show mastery in a skill, it doesn't keep quizzing them.

No Red Ink also has writing prompts that could offer you some inspiration. The website has a paid option with more choices and content, but so far, I've used the free version and been very impressed.

Wattpad

Before discussing this site, I always give my students a disclaimer about internet safety. Wattpad is essentially a social media community for writers and readers. You can go on and publish your poems, stories, and books, either all at once or serially. Others can read and comment on your work. Some authors have been picked up by Wattpad, so it is an exciting venture for students. It can be a great tool for students to use in order to get more feedback and start thinking about publishing.

Storyboard That!

This is essentially a storyboarding website or comic strip maker. It's a fun way to allow students to get a break from paper and pencil. This is also a nice option to modify lessons for students with special needs in your class. It gives them so many fun customization options, and they still get to tell their story. It's also great to use with the dialogue unit.

It does take some getting used to, so I recommend trying it out yourself first and then teaching students how to use it. The free option can create issues for students to print and save due to a watermark, but we were able to show the final products on the board.

The Hemingway Editor (hemingwayapp.com)

This free tool is a great way to show students how readability affects their storytelling. In creative writing, we use this on paragraphs here and there to help students clean up too many adverbs, passive voice, and confusing sentences. I think using this all the time would stifle creativity and voice. However, it's a great tool for showing students how to think about the impact of their sentence structures.

Spark Creativity Blog

Betsy's blog is an amazing place to find creative ideas for your classroom, both in the writing classroom and the regular content classroom. I subscribe to her emails because she always has so many fun ideas that involve artwork, creative thinking, and expression. Visit her blog at nowsparkcreativity.com to find all sorts of inspiration. I love the One Pager idea she has and have adapted it for the writing classroom as well.

Movies I love to show:

Stonehearst Asylum

As you'll see in Strategy 8, I like to mix up my lessons with other activities such as movies and games. This has been a fan favorite for years because it has an epic twist ending. It gives us a lot of room to discuss things like foreshadowing, twist endings, and suspense.

Warning: Definitely watch this movie first as it isn't right for all audiences. There is a lot of violence, some dark themes, a few archaic swear words, and some scenes that suggest female harm. Commonsense Media is a website that will break down all of the inappropriate parts for you as well (If you don't know about that website, check it out! I use it for any new movie I want to introduce). You need to make sure you are comfortable with it and your students are mature enough to handle it. Even if you don't use it in the classroom, it's so good just for you to watch.

The Illusionist

This movie is an oldie, which is partially why I love to show it. The students haven't seen it, so again, we can evaluate the twists and plot devices in the storyline. There is a disturbing scene at the end, so you do need to make sure you are okay with showing that. Otherwise, it offers a lot of great talking points for a mature audience.

The Village

This older movie tends to be one that students haven't seen as well and offers that deep twist of an ending. It gives you a lot to discuss as far as symbolism, plot devices, and suspense. It has a horror vibe to it but isn't absolutely terrifying, so this is a perfect classroom pick.

J.K. Rowling: Magic Beyond Words

This biographical drama is my favorite for writing class, by far. It follows the true story of J.K. Rowling and her tumultuous rise to fame. This movie starts out feeling a little cheesy, but my students always get wrapped up in it. It's a story about overcoming challenges and finding your passion. I love to show this to aspiring authors because it demonstrates that you really do have to stick with it. J.K. Rowling was not an overnight success, which the movie definitely highlights. This movie is a great forerunner to a unit on publishing and how to keep your head in the game; I find, though, that it inspires students who have all different dreams.

Coraline

This creepy little movie based on the book by Neil Gaiman always intrigues my students. The writing students especially are drawn to the quirky storyline. It leaves a lot of room at the end for discussion of symbolism and plot techniques. Plus, it's really interesting to look at some behind-the-scenes videos on Youtube that show just how involved the process of stop-motion filmmaking is.

The Takeaway:

- Use technology, movie, and books to mix up your classroom learning.

- You don't need fancy prompts in order for students to get inspired.

- Be on the lookout for quality writing you can share with your students. Examples of solid writing can be inspiration on their own.

Strategy Five: Recognize Your Strengths and Weaknesses

One of the hardest parts of teaching creative writing is feeling out your own vulnerabilities, strengths, and weaknesses. Writing, as I've said before, takes courage at any age. Most good writers face the ugly monster of self-doubt. Teaching, as you know, requires a whole other level of confidence. To be in the front of the class teaching about a topic seems to require an expertise that is much higher. Thus, it is really easy to get in your head as a writing teacher and question whether you are truly the person to be instructing others.

I can tell you that no matter what you've accomplished or what writing expertise you have, there will come a point in your teaching of writing you question your worth. I have over twenty novels published and am a USA Today Bestselling author—and I still doubt my worth in front of the class. Am I really skilled enough to teach about writing? Do I really know what's best? Even when I tell myself my years of experience and knowledge are serving the kids well, the voice of self-doubt creeps in. *Yes, but you aren't Stephen King good. Yes, but you aren't a NYT bestselling author.*

I mention this because I want you to know that self-doubt in writing and, thus, in teaching writing is par for the course. It doesn't matter how much experience you have or don't have. You will wonder if you are teaching the right thing. It doesn't help that creative writing is so subjective. When J.K. Rowling wrote under her penname and submitted to publishers after amassing titles and wealth from *Harry Potter,* publishers rejected her work. If J.K. Rowling's work is getting rejected, then that should tell you that the industry is truly subjective.

So what's the answer? I think it's twofold.

First, you need to recognize your strengths in writing. Yes, you have them. Even if you have never written, you have strengths. Take some time to explore them. What topics do you feel passionately about when it comes to writing? If you had to write something today, what would you write? What genre and medium would you use? Thinking back to your own schooling, what types of writing did you do well on?

Knowing what you are good at can help give you the confidence you need in other areas. I would recommend starting with a unit on the topic you are most confident in if it's your first year. This allows you to explore the structure and style of your teaching while still covering a topic that needs to be taught.

After you've figured out your strengths, you also need to figure out what you struggle with. For me, I have a hard time figuring out how to teach poetry. There are so many types, and it's just a different way of thinking than prose. How do I break it down for students while still giving them creative freedom? It's definitely the area I feel least confident in, along with science fiction.

Once you know your weakest areas, your job is to consider resources to help you. I'm not just talking about books and activities. Think about reaching out to experts in the field.

Authors, for the most part, are the kindest, most giving group of people I know. Most love talking about books and their work, especially with aspiring writers. I've done numerous Google Hangouts with authors big and small. I think the more voices you can let your students hear from the field, the better. Search for smaller and mid-sized authors who might have the time in their schedule to meet with your students. Look for local writing groups in your area or even college professors. Take the time to reach out for help in the areas you don't feel confident in. Not only will this take the pressure off of you, but it will help your students hear multiple perspectives on the subject. I think the more approaches they hear, the more likely they are to find one that clicks for them since we all approach writing differently.

If you can't find any authors or poets who will meet with you directly, Ted talks are another great place to look. I really like the one by Elizabeth Gilbert on the muse, but there are countless more that can help inspire your students. It's okay to let someone else do the talking if you don't feel confident enough to do so.

Furthermore, don't be afraid to be honest with your students. We talk a lot in my class about strengths and weaknesses. We talk about leaning into your writing weaknesses because that's how we grow. Be upfront with them if you don't feel like an expert in an area. Then, let them see you trying to expand your skills. Let them see you experiment with different mediums and genres. Be brave enough to share your progress or lack of along the way. Do some of the activities with them, and share your work. Show them writing really is a practice and a process. What better way for them to gain the confidence to explore their own weaknesses than by seeing you work on yours?

Writing teachers don't need to be Stephen King famous. They don't need to be published or recognized. They don't have to be experts at writing. They simply have to be open minded enough to encourage creativity, empathetic enough to create a safe atmosphere, and passionate enough about the subject to make the students understand the truth we're all here trying to prove: creative writing matters.

The Takeaway:

- It's natural to doubt yourself when it comes to being a writing teacher.

- Start with your strongest subject or topic when you are teaching for the first time.

- Don't be afraid to ask for help teaching topics you struggle with.

- Many writers will be willing to meet with your class via Zoom or Google for free.

- Be honest with your students about your weaknesses and show them how you are working on them.

● Writing is about growth. Model that for your students.

● You don't need publishing credentials or successes to be a successful writing teacher.

Strategy Six: Creating effective critique circles is crucial.

You may think the activities and direct instruction you do in creative writing class are the most crucial and where learning takes place. To an extent, this is, of course, true. However, I would argue the most beneficial aspects of the class happen during sharing. As long as you've created an effective system of critique circles, your students will do most of their growing on days when they are listening to others' work.

I've come to learn most students have never really read their peers' writing. They have no idea what others are doing, and they have no clue where their writing ranks with others. This is not to say writing is about comparison. However, I do think there is a lot of self-worth and self-understanding that takes place by realizing how your work differs from others.

As teachers, we read so many writings from students. Thus, we forget the fact that most students don't get the same opportunity. Thus, I think sometimes teachers undervalue the concept of sharing. What could be learned from students hearing others' work? And isn't the teacher the expert in the room? Shouldn't they be the only one offering feedback?

Having students share their writing, however, serves many benefits. First, students are opened up to the various styles of writing and of seeing the world. They get a better appreciation for different approaches to thinking, creating, and drafting their ideas. This exposure to different concepts and styles is valuable in itself. Second, students can learn about their peers in new ways. There is a deeper connection that is forged when you hear someone's take on the world, no matter what subject they are writing about. Hearing another student's ideas in creative writing helps them appreciate their peers for the unique individuals they are and enhances the community building you are working on.

Furthermore, students will be of different skill levels in your class. It is crucial for your students to hear what makes writing good. By hearing other writing and then, most importantly, discussing the strengths and weaknesses of it, students begin to internalize what effective creating writing looks like. As they hear what excites readers and understand sections of the writings that are lackluster, they can begin to mimic these tactics in their own work.

Finally, critique circles teach students to be attentive listeners and readers. By really helping students focus on how something is written, they begin to critique detailed elements of works, not just in your class, but in everything they do. This awareness for the written word and its power can open up new learning doors in every subject they encounter.

Critique circles are my favorite days of writing class. We get a glimpse into each student's mind, and we also get to bear witness to each student's growth. It's a beautiful thing to see a student who lacks creativity or knowledge in the area flourish. It's exciting to see students who sometimes struggle in the core classes hit it out of the park in writing class.

We all want to be seen. Creative writing class critique circles give everyone a chance to shine. But how do you set them up so they are effective and students utilize them to the best of their ability? Here are some tips I've used to make sure my critique days are my students' favorite as well.

The Format of a Share Day

In general, this is the approach I take to a share day:

- I ask for volunteers first, especially at the beginning.

- I move to random selection using a Name Generator Wheel online (the students love this, and it makes it more fun).

- Students come up front to our "share chair." This should be a "special" chair used for sharing.

- Students read their work to the class. I sit near the back and take notes on their work.

- Students in the class first talk about strengths of the piece/things they like. I let students talk first, and then I give my feedback out loud as well. This allows students to hear my advice on every piece and learn from every piece.

- Students then ask any questions they have or give advice for how to make the piece stronger.

- I give students my notes sheet so they have written commentary they can keep.

All of the grading happens right here. This frees me up grading wise and allows students to really understand what we are looking for. Grades are mostly for participation and effort anyway.

Skills to Teach Students Before Your First Critique

It is imperative that students understand HOW to critique before you have your first critique circle. I let students know from day one that the power of the class is in their hands. A group of students who are unwilling to offer honest critiques guarantees the class will be boring. We discuss on the first day of class a few key points for critique circles:

- Honesty is key. We have to be willing to tell our peers what doesn't work. If we just say "great job" for everything, the class loses its meaning and power.

- There is always something positive and something negative about each piece. Having negatives about your piece doesn't discount it.

- Make it clear to your students that accepting criticism as a writer is a crucial step. However, it is also a balancing act. It's a subjective field, so you have to begin to understand as a writer when to listen to your readers' criticism and when to stick to your gut.

This is a skill I work on with them individually and push them to understand as the semester goes on.

On the day of our first critique, we review these concepts. I also lay out expectations for the class:

- Everyone must participate in critiques. If I have a class where students refuse to be a part of it, I do have them fill out critique sheets. I try to just do this verbally, though, on the first day and see where we stand. Usually, the students are willing to buy into the critique process, and it can remain very informal. I think this adds to the comfort level and environment.

- Kindness is important. You must be honest, but you can do so in a kind way.

- Every piece has value, even if it needs work.

- There are no phones, other work, or distractions when someone shares. It takes bravery to share, and they need to appreciate that.

I also work really hard to model these behaviors while listening. When students give effective feedback, they get praised as well. As your sense of community builds as well, students will be more apt to give honest, effective feedback.

Supporting Nervous Students

There will undoubtedly come a time when you have a student who, for one reason or another, refuses to share. As sharing is a crucial part of growth and development in this class, I try my best to encourage these students to share. Usually, once they share their first piece, they realize it isn't absolutely terrifying. I've had students who were shaking on the first share circle volunteer to go first after a few weeks.

Sometimes, students are fine with their work being shared; they are just nervous about reading aloud in front of the class. In these cases, I allow students to pick someone else to read their work for them. They must still be in the room to hear the work read and the critiques. This can take off the pressure at first for students who are nervous.

If you have a student, though, who will not share, there are some tactics you can take. I do have in my syllabus that students lose 10% of their points if they refuse to share an assignment unless they have spoken to me first. Sometimes, writing takes students to very personal places. If students have a piece they can't share due to that reason, as long as they communicate with me, I am understanding and lenient about it. I have had students over the years, though, who simply refuse to share because they don't want to participate in the class. This is why I instituted the 10% rule. Otherwise, you run the risk of the whole class deciding they don't want to share, and I promise you, a class without sharing is going to be very boring. It becomes another English class essentially because the magic of the class really does come through critiques and feedback.

Another tactic I've used with students who have severe anxiety or other situations is to challenge them to a compromise. I set a realistic goal for them: by the end of the marking period, share two pieces. They still must turn their work into me, and I do grade them that way. However, setting this goal for students can take some of the pressure off while still working towards your ultimate goal of sharing.

Don't be surprised, either, if a student who is reluctant to share at the beginning of the class becomes more open as the sense of community builds. This is why building a safe community in my classroom is my number one priority when I start a writing class. The benefits of doing so trickle into every other strategy in a positive way.

Problems that can arise

Even in your best class, issues can still arise on critique days. Being prepared to handle them, like anything in teaching, is your best line of defense.

Some students don't lack a sense of confidence when they come into your class. These students sometimes will feel they are experts in their field and have nothing to learn. They might argue and get defensive about every single critique offered in the class.

Usually, I pull these students aside and have a very frank conversation about how no one is perfect in writing. I share my own experiences of editing in publishing and how being a good writer is understanding there are always ways to grow. We talk about having trust in the other students to offer advice. We also discuss how even though they don't have to take every suggestion, they do have to listen to the ideas respectfully.

Sometimes, you will have students who are really harsh on other students' writing. This can really kill the confidence you are working so diligently to build. Again, I find honest conversations with the student one-on-one can be helpful in combating this issue.

Sensitive topics can arise in a share circle. We discuss this possibility early in the class. We discuss the importance of being open-minded because ideas might be shared that you disagree with, and that is okay. If you build a successful community feel, you'll find students are very kind, generous, and empathetic towards each other. I do make it very clear at the beginning of the year we are still governed by school rules even though it is a creative writing class. Students know they cannot write anything that could be threatening or perceived as a threat. They are not allowed to write about other students in their work. I do allow cursing as long as it is for character building or has a purpose in the plot; I tell students that if they get called on it, they must be able to explain why the word was necessary. I find this approach keeps them from using them just for the sake of using them.

You will still have students who share things that are very personal or alarming. Be prepared to go to guidance frequently for your class, as writing often stirs up deep feelings and hardships. I truly think this is a good thing. The fact that students have seen my class as a safe place to ask for help or to reach out is, in my opinion, a compliment to the community we've built. Just know you will need to be prepared to reach out to school administrators for help based on your school policies and procedures. When in doubt if something should be reported, I always err on the side of caution.

Ways to Mix Up Your Circles

One of the biggest killers of creativity, I think, is routine. We talked about not falling into a write share pattern. I also think from time to time, it is good to mix up your sharing routine. If you have a huge writing class, it might not be feasible for everyone to share with the whole class every single time. I do think there is value in everyone hearing every other student's work at least one time. However, if you have a huge class, there are other tactics you can use to mimic the critique circles.

Sometimes, I pair students up for one-on-one critiquing. I save this for later in the class when they are comfortable with each other. This allows students to get through a work in a period, and it allows them to take a close look at their peers' work. I do sometimes use critique sheets for this.

I also sometimes split the class in half and let them run their own mini critique circle. This again cuts down on the time it takes to share and takes some pressure off of your students who don't like sharing in front of the whole class.

If you've done a shorter piece (I love doing 100-word stories because they are challenging and help students learn to be concise), you can create a gallery walk for students. They walk around and read at their leisure, writing comments on a comment sheet by each one.

There are a multitude of ways you can accomplish sharing and critiquing work. I think the key is that you create an atmosphere where it is taking place and find ways to have every voice heard.

The Takeaway:

- When done well, critique circles are what will lead to student growth. Students learn what makes writing exciting or lackluster and can begin to mimic techniques of others.

- Sharing aloud allows students to bond, hear ideas, and examine other unique styles of writing.

- Every piece has good and bad about it. Make sure your students focus on both.

- Honesty is the most important element of sharing. Make sure students aren't just telling each other "good job."

- Teach students how to critique. Help them take ownership of the class by assisting each other.

• Some students will be hesitant to share, but offer encouragement and compromise when you need to.

• Mix up your sharing through various formats, including groups and partners

Strategy Seven: How to tackle writer's block

No matter how exciting your activities are or how close-knit your students are, there will come a time in the class that the dreaded occurrence will take place: writer's block.

It might be the whole class just loses their creative mojo. Perhaps it will be a student or two who chronically just can't get the writing done. As a teacher, it can be so difficult to navigate this tricky territory because writer's block is a real thing. Still, you need to teach students to overcome it or your whole class will teeter.

From Stephen King to novice writers, everyone faces a time when their creativity is lacking. Perhaps you've felt it yourself. The stresses of life, illness, lack of confidence, loss, boredom, monotonous days–they can all play into a lack of imagination and creativity. Couple that with creeping thoughts of "I can't do this" or "My writing isn't good," and you have a recipe for writing disaster.

How, then, can you help maneuver your students past this dreaded cliff of paralysis? How can you help them find their way to the other side where creativity once again flows?

It isn't easy, but nothing is in teaching or writing. Here are some of my tried-and-true tips, though, for helping get the writing flowing again–because without writing, well, the whole concept of a writing class is pretty much impossible.

1. **Normalize writer's block but don't use it as an excuse**

We discuss writer's block openly in my class because, as I've stated, it is a real thing. We talk about the causes of it and how every writer deals with it. The TED talk by Elizabeth Gilbert is great because she talks about it in her video, and Stephen King mentions it in his book.

However, when we discuss writer's block, we also discuss how it isn't a valid excuse. I show them articles and advice from various writers, all of which say the same thing: the cure for writer's block is simply to write.

That truly is it. I know from my own experience that when I'm feeling down and out about my writing or stuck, the secret that fixes it is always just to keep writing. It doesn't have to be good writing or particularly focused writing. It just has to be writing. If I'm writing a book and am stuck, I might take a day to write an article or a social media post. I'll write to a friend. I'll write in a journal. As long as I'm writing, the words get flowing and, before I know it, I'm not drowning in self-doubt anymore.

Students in my class are allowed to have a bad day–everyone is. If they are dealing with a loss or a hard time, they know they can get a reprieve from the assignment. However, they also know I will hold them accountable and not let them fall into the endless swamp that is writer's block. I do not allow them to use excuses on a daily basis of: "I can't write today" or "I only write at home." I do not allow them to use being blocked as an excuse to not write.

They don't have to write awesome things every day. They don't have to like what they are writing. They do, however, have to try.

I also don't let students use the excuse that they only write at home or in a certain spot or fill in the blank. We discuss how J.K. Rowling started writing on a train, and other authors, too, wrote their works in all sorts of places. To be a writer, a true writer, means you can adapt and write anywhere. We practice that idea in my class.

1. Discuss the value of nature when it comes to writer's block

Another key antidote for writer's block is nature. Students might initially think this is cheesy or untrue, but it really does work. Many writers talk about how a walk without technology helped them solve all sorts of plot holes and failing manuscripts.

I don't have to tell you that today's students spend so much time wrapped up in technology, which can be a creativity killer. Without time to be lost in thoughts or bored, students don't have the need to be imaginative–or the space for it.

Encourage your students to get outside, even if it's just a few minutes a day. Better yet, set a few classes outside and encourage free writing. This writing doesn't even have to be collected. The only rule is they have to keep writing for the allotted time. You can also spend some time just sitting outside and allowing students to have time to think. These quiet moments away from technology and distraction often spark the best ideas.

3. Play the "What If" game

Orson Scott Card has an amazing quote I adore: ""Everybody walks past a thousand story ideas every day. The good writers are the ones who see five or six of them. Most people don't see any."

For me, this quote really highlights the idea I try to impress upon my students: stories are everywhere. Every facet of your life holds the potential for beautiful stories to be told. I encourage my students to keep a journal to jot down these ideas or simply to start taking note of them. Many times, the best writing ideas come from observing real life and asking the "What if?" question. This is how many of my own novels came to be.

Overcoming writer's block is really about staying open. We get stuck in a rut in writing sometimes, just like with everything in life. When that happens, the spark dies a bit. Encourage students to stay open minded and to keep looking for the beauty around them. Teach them how to see stories in the mundane, and start looking yourself for things to tell about everything around you.

Once you teach students that writer's block is normal BUT they have the power to overcome it, they will become unstoppable writers, something we're all trying to achieve.

The Takeaway:

- Acknowledge that writer's block happens, but don't allow students to use it as an excuse to not write.

- The best way to get over writer's block is simply to write; teach students how to write even when they lack motivation.

- Sometimes, other creative ventures can help break up writer's block. Encourage students to step away from technology and spend time thinking, especially in nature.

- There is inspiration to be found everywhere. Students need to know how to use the question "What if?" to spark creativity.

Strategy Eight: Talk about your own writing in order to encourage your students.

If you want your students to be inspired in your class to be vulnerable, grow, and learn in the area of writing, you need to follow these guidelines as well. More than any other class, creative writing class is one where you really do need to do the work with the students. Even when you don't think they are, your students are watching what you're doing and modeling you.

I know what you are thinking: I already graduated high school. I've put in my time. I don't need to prove myself. And you are right. All of these are true statements.

However, I have found in creative writing class that students need to see you believe in the mission you are setting before them. They need to really understand it's okay to be open with your writing, that everyone feels nervous to share, and that you do it anyway. More than any other class I teach, this class is about building a community together. The students are a huge part of what you build. Thus, you need to help showcase for them what it means to follow the guidelines you are setting up for them.

I also know some of you may be doubting your worth as writers right now. Maybe you've never been published, or maybe you're brand new to teaching. Perhaps you have been asked to teach this class and don't really feel qualified to teach. Maybe you've never even done any creative writing yourself.

I'm here to tell you that none of that matters, truly. Foremost, I don't care how many titles you accumulate or how many works you publish; you will always feel nervous to share with your students, and potentially, you will always feel like you aren't quite good enough. That's partially because that's the nature of writing. I don't believe there really ever is a thing as an expert in writing. I think that's what makes writing so difficult yet so special at the same time. You are never done with the journey because there is always more to learn and perfect.

Secondly, none of it matters because it really is about growth. Your students don't need Stephen King or J.K. Rowling in front of them in order to do that. They need someone to guide the way, to lay the groundwork for what makes good writing, and to encourage them along the way. More than any other class, this course is so much about just guiding students to finding the answers. You can't figure out who they are as a writer for them. You can't help them learn to fine tune their voice without them doing it themselves. Your job is not to be the expert in the room. Your job is to be a guide and to set good examples for what writers do.

Writers:

1. Experiment with their voice.
2. Take risks with their writing.
3. Write, edit, write, edit–repeat cycle.
4. Learn from what doesn't work in their writing.

5. Self-reflect.
6. Encourage others while being honest.
7. Don't focus on the success of a piece but on being vulnerable and writing from a genuine place.

The more you can model this for students, the better your class will be. This can take on a lot of different formats. You can talk about your writing experiences and pieces you wrote. Don't just talk about your successes, though. Give examples of times you struggled. Share with them times your pieces didn't work. Talk about genres you struggle to write.

From time to time, it's also effective to actually do the assignments you are giving them, even if it's a struggle. I find that struggling through the difficult prompts and letting students see you tackle them can be inspiring to them. Furthermore, don't be afraid to share your work with them. Watching you showcase your vulnerability and uncertainty can also be a really effective motivator.

I know it can be terrifying opening up with your writing. Teachers are already carrying the weight of the world, truly. Teaching has its own pressures, and being in charge of a writing class for the first time is daunting enough. I challenge you, though, to challenge yourself. Step outside of your comfort zone and let your students see you are willing to practice what you tell them to do. The benefits make the struggle worthwhile because as you open up, your students will buy into what you are teaching on a deeper level.

The Takeaway:

- Share your own writing journey, good and bad, with the students

- You don't have to be published or an award-winning writer to showcase your work.

- Be willing to work through the lessons and grow with your students

Strategy Nine: Creativity isn't always found with a paper and pencil.

One of the beautiful things about teaching creative writing is it gives you a unique opportunity within the school setting to focus on a word we don't often get to emphasize: creativity. There are few sanctuaries left in the education system where students can think creatively and use their imagination. Take advantage of this opportunity.

Creativity in your writing class can take on many forms. Don't limit your instruction to paper and pencil or even writing. In my class, one of my units is focused solely on creativity. Students need to learn how to go about generating ideas, how to let their minds free up for possibility, and how to explore. We do this in a variety of ways. I'm listing some of my favorite methods for mixing up the class and encouraging creative thought, but don't limit yourself to these. Really, any activity that gets kids to move out of their seats, to use their brains, to problem solve, to invent, to think of words creatively, or just to dare to dream are valuable, educational initiatives in this kind of class.

Games

Games are my favorite way to break up the monotony that can sometimes plague writing class. If you fall into a routine of writing and sharing, creativity can really fall flat. I've found traditional board games that encourage interaction and creative thinking are a great way to build on skills while getting the students to bond. Some of our favorites are Scattergories, Taboo, and Pictionary. These games encourage vocabulary building and team building in a fun, interesting way.

Drawing/Art Activities

There are close connections between art and writing. Any type of fun or simple craft you can incorporate into your class is a nice way to build creativity and encourage it. It's okay if your students aren't skilled in art–focus on the value of trying something new. Look out for ways you can pair up with the art program in your school. At the end of the year, some of our art classes do installation pieces, and I love having students explore those and even write about them.

Collages, especially centered around words or ideas, are another way students can express ideas in a fun, new way.

Problem-Solving

Anything that makes your students think deeply can help encourage them to dream up new problems and solutions to write about. When I taught a summer writing camp last year, I incorporated riddles for students of all ages to encourage deep thinking. I also love doing brain teasers and creative thinking activities to promote high-level thought processes. Any word puzzles can also be effective ways to build on creativity.

Community Building activities

Anything you can do to promote students getting to know themselves and each other is bound to heighten the creative experience. I love going on Pinterest and finding fun, appropriate "Would you rather?" questions. At one time, I even took a beach ball and wrote a bunch of these questions on it. When we had spare time in writing class, I would put on some music and have the kids throw the ball around. Whoever holds it when the music stops must answer the question their right thumb is touching. This was a super fun way to get everyone involved and to get to know each other on a deeper level.

I've also had days where I have students write deep, thought-provoking questions on notecards. I pick them out at random and have students answer them.

Sometimes, even simple conversations can create discussion. Once your class feels comfortable, you'll find that they are more open to asking questions, talking about their favorite things, or pondering over deeper topics. Some classes, we simply have conversations for the entire period, which to me is a beautiful thing. Conversations stir thought, and thinking in a different way can inspire great ideas for writing. In many classes, you are guided by the constraints of a limited amount of time to move through huge amounts of curriculum. I've found that in writing class, I can go at a more leisurely pace and take pauses in the curriculum for things the students are interested in. Thus, encourage students to talk, to get to know each other, and to have fun.

Movies

I've already mentioned some of the academic movies I recommend, but I mention this again here because movies are a wonderful way to:

- Infuse your class with fun

- Help students relax when they are running out of steam

- Encourage analysis from a writer's perspective of plots, characterization, and ideas

- Help students relax into your class.

I like to show "fun" movies that students can kick back for. For example, my writing students love the movie *Coraline*, so we take a few days to watch it, eat snacks, and discuss what works from a storyline perspective. Teaching students to analyze movies from a writer's eye is a valuable skill. Thus, after your class, every movie they watch can be a springboard or a teacher for good versus flawed writing. Moreover, the chance to really relax and watch a movie together can also free the mind from self-doubt, pressures of coming up with ideas, and boredom. I find after a few "breaks" in the curriculum, we come back to the next writing assignment more excited and ready to work.

The Takeaway:

- Building creative writing skills doesn't have to be limited to the page. Don't be afraid to infuse your class with fun activities that help students develop creativity.

• Any time you can build connections with your students, do it, even if it slows down your pace of the class.

• Don't underestimate the value of talking–really talking. Encourage open conversations that make students think and connect in new ways.

• Games and movies can still be educational but are a fun way to give students a break. Creativity demands a reprieve from the action sometimes.

• There are few other courses in the school day where creativity is a valuable, essential part of the curriculum. Use that to your advantage to encourage fun activities, free thought, and imagination.

Strategy Ten: Celebrate students' successes.

Your writing class's goal is not just to teach students how to be confident writers and how to develop the most sought-after skills in the industry; your class should also be a place where writers are celebrated. Few other places in a school building provide the opportunities for students to receive accolades for writing. Thus, I try to make sure students get the adequate attention and praise for their stand-out pieces.

Remember that for some of your writing students, their skillset doesn't lend itself to trophies, showy moments, or recognition. For your writers who are not interested or involved in other activities, there are few chances for them to be applauded for their work.

This is another reason why I put so much weight on sharing in my class. Yes, it is a chance for students to learn what to do better. More than that, though, it's a chance for students to show off the work they put so much heart and soul into. It's a chance for students who sometimes feel like they are on the backburner of the school to have a moment in the spotlight.

Within my classroom, I have a star writing wall. This is simply a place where I have six clipboards hung up with command strips. There is a title and a cute border around it. The clipboards allow me to frequently switch out the works that appear there. It's a small gesture, but it's a way for students to have their work read by others outside the class. I do see my students stopping to check out the works there from time to time.

I also have another spot in the classroom where students in my writing class were asked to write inspirational pieces either under their name or anonymously. These are on my door for all to read. The idea is that I wanted students to understand the power they have in their words to impact others.

Any time you can promote your students' work both inside and outside the classroom, I think it is important to do so. I look for opportunities and contests for students to get published frequently.

One of my all-time favorite resources is Young Writers (youngwritersusa.com[1]). They run several contests a year for students in high school. Typically, they run a dystopian contest in the fall that is a 100-word story. I love this story format because students don't feel intimidated by it. Many students will give it a try. The winners of this contest get published in anthologies in the spring and have a chance to win prizes. They also run a poetry contest in the spring where students can also get published. The best part about this organization is that it is free to enter, and they also send you resources as a teacher to make the most out of the contest. I've had several students win a place in the anthology. This not only is a great way for students to be recognized for their work, but it also serves as an amazing resume builder for students looking to pursue writing as a career.

---

1. https://youngwritersusa.com/

Another favorite contest of mine is the Scholastic Writing Awards. This is a national contest that is very prestigious. It does cost to enter, although the fee is very minimal. The awards for this contest make the entry fee worthwhile. I have had one student win an award in this contest, and again, it's a great resume builder.

There are many other opportunities that will come up during the year if you keep your eyes open. We have several local contests that come up during the year. I also encourage my students to enter any essay writing contests for scholarships because many students won't take the time to do so.

Another place I like to promote with my students is Wattpad. This reading and writing community is a great place to extend the walls of your classroom. Students can get feedback from readers and share their work with the world in a relatively safe environment. I've found those on Wattpad to be welcoming, professional, and appropriate. However, you should warn your students that like every online space, there are trolls and also dangers. Be sure to discuss internet safety with students, and I always encourage them to talk to their parents before signing up for the platform. Nonetheless, there are numerous opportunities for growth, recognition, and even publishing that can come from the platform.

If you teach seniors, there are many websites that accept submissions. One of my favorites for female writers is *Harness Magazine.* They welcome articles on what it means to be female, and they are also one of the few online publications I know of that accepts poetry. I love their mission and their platform for submitting. They do not pay, but I find it is a great jumping off point for students hoping to do more article writing and get their work out there.

I always make sure to teach my students safety when it comes to publishing. We discuss some of the basic rules:

- Other than reputable contests, you should not pay anyone to publish your work.

- Do not share sensitive information online.

- Research the publications to make sure they are legitimate.

- Be sure that if you publish a piece, you will be able to handle criticism because people online can be cruel.

If your student happens to get published or win a contest, be sure to contact administration to let them know. I like for these students to know that what they are doing matters, even if it is not a widely recognized or celebrated field sometimes.

The Takeaway:

- Your writing class isn't just a class; it is a place to celebrate writing.

- Recognize your students' hard work as often as possible in a genuine way.

- Keep your eyes open for any opportunity that can allow students to share their work with a wider audience.

- Create spaces in your classroom to share student work and give them more readers.

- Teach students about safety when it comes to publishing and submitting pieces.

- Coordinate with your administration to recognize writing achievements big and small.

Strategy Eleven: Focus on Growth, Not Mastery

As we've discussed over and over by this point, creative writing class is a different model than most of the classes you've probably taught before. Mostly, this comes from the subjective nature of the class. Further, I think this class has different requirements because of my approach to it; my focus is solely on building confidence an openness in my writers. I want them to be sure footed in their pursuit of their writing voice while also willing to take risks.

Because of my goals, my writing class is not graded on mastery. I do not make lofty promises to turn them into John Green or J.K. Rowling or any other famous writer. I do not require that they "fit any molds" when it comes to writing either. Thus, my grading and assessments do not focus on those goals, either.

Instead, I've found that grading for growth instead of mastery is appropriate in this course. What does that look like? To be honest, it looks a lot less stressful and data-driven than some educational institutions might prefer. Still, each writer in my class is not being held to the same standard. They are, instead, competing with themselves. I want them to leave the class feeling like they're better than they were when they stepped in; I want that improvement to also be discernible in their storytelling.

For the most part, in level one, students are graded on participation in the beginning. As long as they are trying and meeting basic page requirements, they get the points. Their feedback comes through critique circles and suggestions, but they are never penalized for writing a piece that "didn't work." What does that mean, anyway? Plus, as an educator and author, I still don't think I'm qualified to analyze that lofty sentiment.

As the year progresses, their grades are based on growth. When they get feedback, I want to see that they are either following the advice or able to rationalize why the advice isn't fitting for their writing voice; either outcome is sufficient for me. I do push students who think their writing is perfect to consider classmates' suggestions, especially when they are getting the same comments over and over. This is where building trust and community is valuable.

We do have rubrics we use at the end of units after students have time to practice the skills we are working on. I use the narrative writing rubric endorsed by my state, but you can design your own. I like to use the same rubric throughout the year, though, so we are working towards consistent goals.

Even with a rubric, though, I am very lenient in this class. Realize you will have students of all levels starting out with you. The challenge as an educator is to assess them based on their willingness to learn, effort, and improvement. As I've mentioned before, I fail to believe there is such a thing as a perfect writer. To require our students, thus, to achieve that vision is, quite frankly, asinine.

I find this lower pressure assessment model improves creativity. Students aren't worried about being wrong and, thus, will take more risks in their writing. They'll compose a poem when they've never even thought of trying to before. They'll write a different genre or a different point-of-view. Take away the fear of failure in your students and you'll see something magical, something I feel saddened to say we rarely see in the classroom lately–a true internal desire to learn, to try, and to explore. I find the students are eager to write, to complete assignments, and to excel.

I've seen students who typically only get failing grades flourish in my class because suddenly, the red pen isn't an enemy to avoid. I've seen confidence soar because the focus is on what they're doing well and on trying, not on being perfect. I've seen Honors and AP students breathe a sigh of relief that percentages and honor roll aren't at stake; they exhale on the way in the class, something they don't get to do all day.

Our class, thus, is still a place of learning and growing. It's still a place where skills are mastered and improved upon. It is not, however, a place of ranking, of competition, or where percentages drop because of failed outcomes. Students do know, however, they have to put in effort. I have had students fail the course for refusing to work or try. My expectations are that while you are in class, you will give it a try. The outcome isn't as important as the practice you put in.

It's a place where we can see learning at its finest, where we can really pursue what I think education should be about–we can give students the freedom and desire to try new ventures, to work on their craft, to fall down, to get back up, and to eventually find a sense of self-worth because they realize they are capable.

How do you put a grade on that?

The Takeaway

- This is not the place for your red pen, super strict grading, or competition. Grade based on effort and growth in order to take the pressure off your students.

- A failed outcome does not equate to a failed grade; so much of writing is about trying things that are risks. Some will work. Some won't. But both types of pieces are valuable to the student and the class.

- Rubrics can help assess growth but use them at the end of units after practice has taken place.

- Recognize all students are starting at a different jumping off point. Honor that with your grading system.

- Determine your focus and goals for the class. Be sure your grading reflects that.

- Writing is subjective. Be sure to set out expectations for students and have fair grading systems that reflect the subjectivity.

- It isn't always about the outcome in this class; it really is about effort and the process of practicing.

A Final Word: The Power of Creative Writing: Inspiration for You

Teaching a creative writing course of any kind can be intimidating and nerve-wracking. I wrote this book for that very reason. I can remember my first year, trying to sort through what to teach, how, and when. There were very few resources on how to actually teach students to write creatively, so I found myself constantly second-guessing myself.

Your first year teaching the class will have its challenges. You'll struggle with your own confidence because, well, creative writing is a vulnerable place to be. You'll sometimes feel emotionally weighed down because of the difficult things your students write. You'll struggle to find adequate, moving inspiration needed in order to inspire others. You'll make mistakes. You'll wonder if you're accomplishing anything at all. You'll wonder if you're the right person for the job.

But here's the thing, dear teacher: you are. You are exactly what your students need.

You're the voice of encouragement in a world that sometimes feels so ugly.

You're the inspiration to achieve greatness in a world that talks so much about odds and statistics.

You're the safe place for students to open up, to share, to create, to take risks, to believe, to imagine, and most importantly, to just be.

Over my years of teaching this course, I've been lucky enough to witness the magic that happens in the walls of a classroom.

I've seen students who feel withdrawn and lonely make friends with students they never would have talked to.

I've seen students tear down their own walls and give their experiences a voice.

I've seen students cry tears of pain, tears of joy, and tears of comfort.

I've seen students console each other, encourage each other, and motivate each other.

I've seen students open up about life-changing experiences we otherwise didn't know about.

I've seen students who thought they couldn't write take ownership for their style and voice.

I've seen students who hate school suddenly not want to miss our class.

I've seen students laugh who haven't laughed for ages.

I've seen a community be forged in the wreckage that public education sometimes feels like.

I've seen students come into their own.

You, dear teacher, are blessed to be at the forefront of this journey for your students. You get to steer the ship. You get to bear witness to these beautiful moments. And along the way, I assure you, you'll have moments, too.

You'll grow and gain confidence. You'll get motivated to work on your own craft and dreams. You'll share and express and connect, something we all go into teaching for.

It really is a class that gives. Unlike any other class, I can honestly say it doesn't even truly matter what skills you teach or don't, or how you approach grading.

What matters is that you give students a place to exhale, to put pen to paper, and to let their minds wander. There are few places like that left in the school or even the world. What a gift you have been given to provide them that refuge.

You are the teacher your students need. You are the teacher who will guide them to these beautiful moments. You are more than worthy of this title.

Now go out there and shine, no matter how you choose to approach this class.

Go out and shine.

Fun Prompts for Students to Answer

1. Tell your favorite childhood memory from the perspective of an object or food.
2. If you could choose any movie or television character to be your boss, who would you choose and why?
3. Write about a dystopian world where a change in weather has created a bleak situation.
4. Write a piece that personifies an emotion you have felt this week.
5. Describe the room you are sitting in using only one-syllable words.
6. Describe the room you are sitting in without using any colors.
7. Write about your morning routine from the perspective of an inanimate object.
8. Write a poem about your favorite number 1-10.
9. Write a rhyming poem about your favorite season.
10. Write a humorous monologue from the greatest invention of all time.
11. Create a new food and describe its magical properties.
12. Describe your favorite outfit from the perspective of the outfit.
13. Imagine one of your favorite cartoon characters was in this class. Write a dramatic scene involving them.
14. Write a scene or story that takes place on an elevator.
15. Write a scene that only uses dialogue and takes place at the last store you were in.

16. Write a scene that uses the words: green beans, a pretzel, a werewolf, and a spork.
17. Write a suspenseful scene that does not include any words that end in -ly.
18. Write a scene that takes place in the forest at night but isn't scary.

Story Starters

1. When he turned back around, he couldn't believe how the entire scene had changed.
2. Doubting herself, she stood with shaky legs to claim what was hers.
3. It's true what they say: Life goes on, even if you aren't ready for it to.
4. I never forgot the way he made me feel that cold, December day.
5. Everything was normal except for the werewolf staring down at me in the middle of hte hall.
6. The crying from behind the door rattled me.
7. I was walking my dog when suddenly, the low growl he emitted made me look up.
8. There is no tomorrow, not in a world like this.
9. Yesterday no longer exists.
10. Beauty has forsaken me once more.
11. You can never know the impact a single word can have until it's too late.
12. They stood beneath the lamp's glow, their eyes saying everything they couldn't.
13. The machine rattled with omnipotent power, but all I could think to do was run.
14. When I approached the clearing that fateful day, I looked down to see a metal object; it was not of this world, though.
15. The words coming out of her mouth were completely foreign as I stood still, trying not to draw attention to

myself.
16. Freedom, as I've come to learn, is more powerful than anything.
17. Her heart raced as she slammed the car door.
18. There was no denying the dread permeating the air between them.
19. Once you leave this town, there truly is no coming back–not alive, anyway.
20. "Don't even think about trespassing in that lot."

About the Author

Lindsay (L.A.) Detwiler is a USA Today Bestselling thriller author, a romance author, and a high school English teacher. During her ten years in the classroom, she has taught three levels of creative writing, was an adjunct English professor, and has also instructed with a private school. Her debut novel, *Voice of Innocence*, released in 2015. Since then, she's published over twenty novels. Her thriller *The Widow Next Door* with HarperCollins UK hit the USA Today Bestseller's list. *The Diary of a Serial Killer's Daughter* was named a Readers' Favorite Bronze Medal Winner for thrillers and was translated into Polish.

She lives in Hollidaysburg, Pennsylvania, with her husband, their six rescue cats, and their Great Dane, Edmund.

For more information, visit:

www.ladetwiler.com[1]

www.instagram.com/ladetwiler[2]

www.facebook.com/ladetwiler[3]

Or email her at:

authorladetwiler@gmail.com

---

1. http://www.ladetwiler.com

2. http://www.instagram.com/ladetwiler

3. http://www.facebook.com/ladetwiler

Lindsay's Books
Sweet Romance

Voice of Innocence

Without You

Remember When

Then Comes Love

Where Love Went

Inked Hearts

Wild Hearts

Hidden Hearts

Lone Hearts

Texan Hearts

Promised Hearts

All of You

Still Us

Who We Were

To Say Goodbye

The Trail to You

No Time for Promises

Falling for the Farmer

Thriller/Horror

The Flayed One

The Redwood Asylum

The Diary of a Serial Killer's Daughter

A Tortured Soul

The Arsonist's Handbook

The One Who Got Away

The Widow Next Door

Her Darkest Hour

The Delivery

Evette

Tell Me All Your Lies

Poetry

She (Is?) Loved

She (Is?) A Star-Filled Sky

She (Is!) A Warrior-Sunrise

Soft Edges

Did you love *Teaching High School Creative Writing*? Then you should read *She (Is?) A Star-Filled Sky* by Lindsay Detwiler and L.A. Henry!

She (Is?) a Star-Filled Sky is a collection of poetry about learning to love yourself. It is about finding the resilience to stand back up and chase your dreams.

From L.A. Henry, a poetry collection about finding the strength to be your truest self. The poems in this collection cover the trials and tribulations of being a woman in modern society and are divided into four sections: self-worth, self-love, self-identity, and self-fulfillment. poems cover topics such as body image, self-awareness, fulfillment, success, recovery, and confidence. These emotional poems tell the story of the modern woman's struggle to find herself and to help other women rise along the way.

If you're looking for inspiration to follow your true life's journey, these poems will be perfect company.